THE ULTIMATE PIZZA MANUAL

MAKE PIZZA LIKE THE PROS... *USED TO!*

by Francesco Brunaldo

Ultimate Culinary Publications

The Ultimate Pizza Manual
MAKE PIZZA LIKE THE PROS... *USED TO!*
by Francesco Brunaldo

Published by Ultimate Culinary Publications
New York, New York

"The Ultimate Pizza Manual" is a trademark of Francesco Brunaldo

ISBN-13: 978-0-9800346-5-3

For comments, corrections, and questions:

authors@ultimateculinarypublications.com

Neither the author nor the publisher are associated with
any brands or stores mentioned in this book,
nor are they associated with any pizzerias, products,
or other culinary services with similar names or titles.

DISCLAIMER

This book is designed to provide information discovered by extensive research and testing over many years. It is presented with the understanding that the publisher and author are not engaged in rendering professional advice or services.

It is not the purpose of this book to provide all possible variations in recipes or techniques. You should read all the material in this book, as well as other available information.

The information contained in this book is current as of the publication date. Every effort has been made to make this book as accurate as possible. However unlikely, there might be typographical, formatting, or graphical errors or errors or omissions in content.

The purpose of this book is to educate and entertain. Your results might differ, possibly because of non-NYC water. The publisher and author are not liable or responsible for any damages alleged to have resulted from the information in this book.

ABOUT THE AUTHOR

Francesco Brunaldo, whose secret identity as *Pizza Man* is known only to a few close friends, has been eating pizza in New York City for many decades. Suspicious and disgruntled and about the disappearance of real New York City-style pizza and its covert replacement by an evil, rubbery, burnt imposter, he created this secret identity to rescue and restore to the world true, well-made, old-fashioned thin-crust Italian pizza.

Armed with nothing more than an advanced degree in engineering, Brunaldo locked himself in a secret cave and didn't come out until he made hundreds of pizzas and cracked the secret code of now-extinct New York Italian pizza-makers.

CONTENTS

"If it isn't to-die-for

then why bother?"

—Francesco Brunaldo

WHY MAKE YOUR OWN PIZZA?

* IT'S FUN!
* IT'S THE ULTIMATE COMFORT FOOD!
* YOU CAN'T GET REAL NEW YORK CITY PIZZA ANYMORE, ANYWHERE (INCLUDING IN NYC)!

IF YOU'RE NOT MAKING REAL NYC PIZZA
—AT HOME—
YOU DON'T KNOW WHAT YOU'RE MISSING!

I totally love pizza. I think everyone does. Even a friend of mine who lives on a nearly 100% liquid diet will show up for pizza.

I can't live without pizza. I'm Italian-American and I've been eating pizza since my childhood in The Bronx where my Mother taught me everything she knows about cooking and baking. But she never made her own pizza. (Oh, she did make English muffin pizzas which were great...next book!)

My earliest pizza memories are about running a couple of blocks to the take-out pizza parlor on *Crotona Avenue* in Little Italy in the Bronx for a $1.25 pizza. No...that's <u>not</u> $1.25 per slice; that's $1.25 **FOR A WHOLE PIE!** *And* it was large—very large...*And* it was ITALIAN...*And* it had a **VERY THIN** crust... *AND IT WAS SQUISITO!**

I'm grown up and living in Manhattan now and there are several problems with getting pizza in New York City—or *anywhere*:

1) Real Italian pizzerias (with real Italian pizza artisans) are **virtually non-existent.** (I can't find them.)

2) **Cheese** is **way too thick**, heavy, and gummy now. They are definitely not using real mozzarella. I know mozzarella.

3) **Not enough sauce** (not very good anyway), so the pizzas are too dry, besides being too heavy, too thick, and too gummy.

4) **Then there is the crust:** Under-baked or over-baked and burnt. Many pizzerias and even "top-rated" pizza restaurants fail to clean their ovens so you get all the delicious ash from hundreds of burnt pizzas that came before.

5) **Prices have gone through the roof** for what is one of the cheapest things to make. You're getting ripped off; they know you don't know any better.

*Delicious / excellent / exquisite!

Now you can make pro NYC pizza at home!

6) Size Matters / What You See Is Not What You Get. Pizzas are smaller than ever for the high prices they ask *and the pizza you see on the counter for slices is **much larger** than the one you'll get when you order a whole pie*. Tricky. (Before making my own, I learned to buy the ready-made counter pie freshly made for slices; they charge the same so as not to admit the size difference...and...***no waiting***. They don't like this idea. Anyway...You can now make a large pizza yourself at home.)

In my opinion, it's the ultimate comfort food...but **it has to be good** and shouldn't cost a fortune.

The chain pizza places? Can be tasty, but they **do not** make *real*, old-fashioned, New York Italian, thin-crust pizza. And they play lots of games with pricing deals: TV offers, coupons, online pricing, phone pricing. If you don't call and say the secret words (literally), you pay full price, and a paltry 12" pizza (which comes 10") can end up costing you $20 or more—plus a large tip demanded by the delivery person. As of this writing, Domino's pizza has two different "on-line coupons" for 3 medium, 1-topping pizzas: one is for $7.00 each and one is for $5.55 each (the TV offer). Why would you need to click an on-line coupon and then even guess which one?

In short, a pizza in New York is a very scary experience on so many levels. This evolved like this because most people don't know what they're missing. They're too young, too-not-Italian, and too-not-old New York. It takes a good Italian pizza artisan to make a good, Italian pizza and a good old Italian New Yorker to know a good pizza...and a good price. (There's no way I'm going to pay upwards of $3 for a single slice.)

SETTLING FOR SECOND BEST

Having given up on finding a good thin-crust Italian pizza around here, I tried a very nice "Chicago-Style" pizza restaurant nearby. It was excellent (for what it was) and the place had take-out and delivery *and* a very cozy old Chicago-Style atmosphere with Tiffany lamps and photos on the brick walls for dining in. It became one of our favorites.

Then they closed down to make way for yet another high-rise apartment building: more people, less pizza. (More bars opened up, though. Hmmm.)

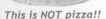

"THAT'S IT! I'M MAKING MY OWN!!" I tried several pizza cookbooks but much was missing and none of those books solved the problem. They were all about "homemade pizza" not *professional* pizza. They called it "pizza," but pizza to me is not just any bread crust with stuff on top. (And it's not tiny.)

This is <u>NOT</u> pizza!!

The reason those other pizza cookbooks don't direct you to making real, professional pizza is because they know making real, professional pizza is normally impossibly difficult. There are trade secrets, equipment and special ingredients involved, and most importantly, most people simply don't know how to do it and try to make it too easy.

Make no mistake about it, making real pizza takes *a little skill and a little practice— **but totally worth it and totally doable at home if you know a few secrets and tricks!***

I'm going to show you ***how to make a very special, incredibly delicious, professional, old-world New York, large-diameter, thin-crust, Italian-style pizza at home relatively easily and cheaply from scratch*** (not just an overly-simplified imitation).

You will learn old-world professional secrets and tricks AND my ultimate pizza sauce recipe...all of which contribute to the making of the ultimate cheese pizza.

You're going to be making the ultimate pizza in two main steps: First, you will make the very important **dough** in advance of making the pizza. (Some people will tell you that you can buy the dough at the local pizzeria, but please don't. A major part of this book—and pizza-making—is about the quality of the dough; it's crucial to our ultimate pizza and it's fun to make.) Later, you'll assemble and **bake the pizza**.

So, let's get on with making your pizza-making experience as easy and delicious as possible, starting with presenting the hardware and "software" (ingredients) you'll need...

You will want to get a **professional stand mixer** of *at least* 250 watts with a dough hook for kneading the dough. (You *do not* want to do this by hand.) I recommend the KitchenAid "Professional" 6-Quart *bowl-lift* stand mixer (575 watts) because even though it looks like a small amount of dough, with kneading it quickly becomes very elastic. A low-power mixer will be strained and can burn out (and so can you if you knead by hand).

You'll find it useful for many other recipes, like breads, cakes, cookies, and unbelievable homemade whipped cream.

The newer models (shown above left) have a heavier spiral dough hook for kneading dough. This newer dough hook configuration might not have the problem I encountered with the older model which comes with a thinner, *straight* hook (lower left).

With the *straight* hook, every couple of minutes, the dough ends up hugging to, and riding around on the hook, instead of being kneaded by the hook. I used to have to stop the machine every couple of minutes to remove the dough from the hook. But I finally easily solved this problem and I'll tell you how later. This is why I'm recommending the bowl-lift type of mixer; you'll need to be able to raise and lower the bowl.

Technically, you *could* knead the dough by hand, but be warned that a) you *will* be using "high-gluten" flour for the dough which is *much* harder to knead by hand for 15-20 minutes, and, b) it still won't turn out as good as using the machine.

6-QUART STAND MIXER

For preparing any medium or large thin-crust pizza: You will need a "**pizza peel**" to form the pizza crust and slide it onto the "pizza screen" for preparation and baking.

18" PEEL (PADDLE WIDTH; WITH SHORT HANDLE) ($8-$40)

If you want to make individual (12") pizzas, you might want to use a smaller peel which you can get at most retail home kitchen supply stores. To get the larger (18") pizza peel, you will have to shop on the Internet or do an in-person visit or phone order to a professional restaurant supply store that carries pizza equipment and hardware supplies. Even in NYC, these stores are hard to find. I recommend one called "**BARI Restaurant and Pizza Equipment Corp.**" at 240 Bowery in New York City. As a matter of fact, they have a website at: www.bariequipment.com. But note that they DO NOT list on-line all the equipment they carry and you will probably have to call to order or go in person. It's a supermarket of equipment.

For preparing, baking, *and* serving your pizza: You need a **pizza screen** larger than your largest pizza. You can use this for any size pizza, but it goes into your oven, so make sure your oven is deep enough from back to door. (See pp. 32–33.) Again, shop on the Internet for this or at BARI.

19" PIZZA SCREEN ($8)

(Note that I've removed the top oven rack and turned the **bottom rack upside-down and backwards** so that the curved part is in front and out of the way to allow the screen the maximum space on which to sit, front-to-back). To determine the maximum size of the screen, make the bottom rack stick out and close the door slowly on it, pushing it in. Open and measure from the front of the rack to the back of the oven.

19" TRAY

($8)

PIZZA WHEEL

For cutting your pizza: You need a pizza tray larger than your largest pizza and a pizza wheel to cut the pizza into eight slices. While you can leave the finished pizza in the tray for serving. the crust *will* get soggy quickly because it does not permit air to reach the bottom to keep the crust dry (use the screen).

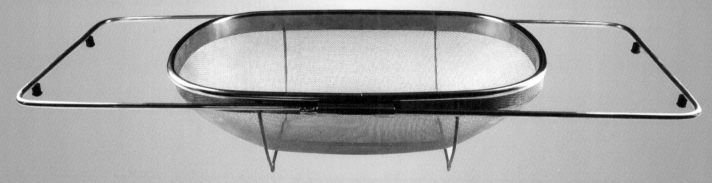

OVER-THE-SINK EXPANDABLE STRAINER ($15)

For holding the pizza screen over the sink: You need an over-the-sink expandable strainer. While you can attempt the fun of making your complete pizza on the peel and slide it right into the oven like the pros, you'd soon find out that's it's near impossible not to mess it up. So you're going to be dressing/topping your pizza dough over the sink because a) your pizza dough will have lot of loose semolina which will fall into the sink, not the oven, b) it's a good height to slide the dough from the peel to the screen for dressing, and c) you'll use it for serving. You can get this on the Internet and at Bed, Bath & Beyond. (Make sure it's wide enough to hang over your sink. Note: If your sink is *small*, you can change the orientation OR put the screen on the counter top instead.)

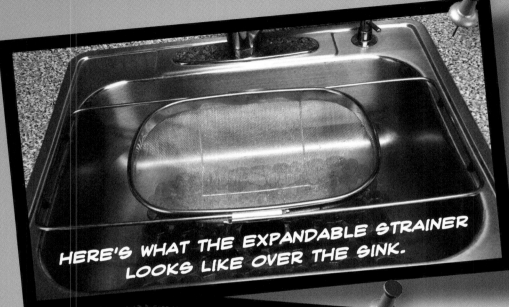

HERE'S WHAT THE EXPANDABLE STRAINER LOOKS LIKE OVER THE SINK.

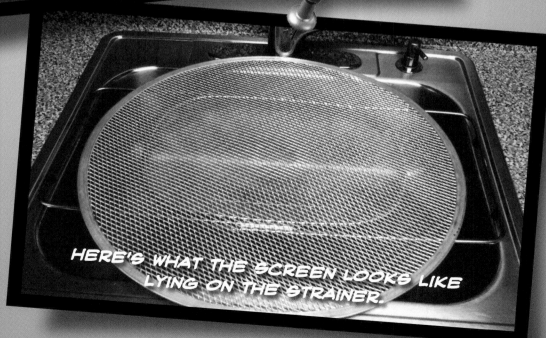

HERE'S WHAT THE SCREEN LOOKS LIKE LYING ON THE STRAINER.

FOOD PROCESSOR OR CHEESE GRATER

For shedding your cheese (mozzarella and, optionally, provolone): I prefer the food processor because it's easy and fast. (Of course, clean up is a pain, for which I use the dishwasher. Alternatively, there's the Zyliss® All-Cheese Grater, with Fine and Coarse Drum Set" (*use coarse*). I don't prefer it because it's *extremely* difficult to handle. You can also try the Magic Bullet® mini blender or just chop by hand.

FLOUR SCOOPER (1-CUP SIZE)

For moving flour from container to scale: It's optional but very convenient. (You're *not* going to be using measuring cups for the flour.)

BOARD SCRAPER

For cleaning your pizza peel... if any dough sticks to your peel. (optional)

12" PLATTER

For moving your dough into the refrigerator: I found this fancy stainless steel 12" platter at "Bed & Bath" on sale for $15. You can use a 12" flat plate or better yet, a 12" standard pizza serving tray. (You'll need something bigger if you make a large deep-dish pizza.)

1-CUP MEASURING CUP & FAST-ACTING STEM THERMOMETER

Available everywhere (but you don't really need the measuring cup)

DOUGH DOCKER

Makes tiny holes in the dough. Available at kitchen stores or on-line (or use a fork).

ACCURATE DIGITAL SCALE AND 3-CUP CONTAINER

For weighing ingredients: The scale should be accurate to one-tenth ounce.

LADLE

For scooping and applying sauce to the dough: You can use a large serving spoon, but a ladle is better.

TWO 2.8 QUART CONTAINERS

For storing your high-gluten flour and semolina: I found these cool "Keeper/Flexible Sealware" containers at the Container Store, although the lids are not very secure. They are just right for a 3-lb bag of flour or semolina.

OXO® BRAND .9 QT "POP" CONTAINER

For airtight storage of yeast: This is a very neat container with a push-button locking lid. I'm going to recommend that you buy a one-pound bag of SAF® "RED" INSTANT YEAST. It will last a long time in this container in the refrigerator, but if you make lots of pizza (and bread), it will go fast. It's the best! (Found at The Container Store®.)

1 QUART CONTAINER

For adjusting height of mixer bowl: This Ziploc® brand container is 2⅛" high which makes it a perfect seat for the mixer bowl to keep it at the proper height (*halfway*) for kneading the dough.

1. HIGH-GLUTEN FLOUR: 14.2% PROTEIN

For some reason, none of the cookbooks or chefs on TV tell you to use HIGH-GLUTEN FLOUR for _real_ pizza. It must be an unspoken trade secret. They'll tell you to use all-purpose flour (10% protein) or bread flour (12.8%), but never high-gluten flour. Real high-gluten ("high-protein") flour is at least 14% protein. **_It's a must_!**

BUT...High-gluten flour is hard to get...even on the Internet...**except** for KingArthurFlour.com (<u>14.2</u>% protein), item #3332:

http://www.kingarthurflour.com/shop/detail.jsp?id=3332

At the time of this writing, flour is "rising" and high-gluten flour is way more expensive...now **$6.25** for a <u>3</u>-pound bag at King Arthur! ($5.50 two months ago.) Compare this to all-purpose flour at 89¢ for a 5-lb bag just a couple of years ago.

If you can find it on the Internet and have the storage space, get a 50 or 100 pound bag. Note that little flour bugs can hatch after a while (trash the bag), but it helps to keep the flour tightly sealed, refrigerated, and/or used up quickly.

 2. SEMOLINA

They also don't tell you about using SEMOLINA for real pizza. Another trade secret. It goes _into_ the dough and _under_ the dough. It's coarse and resembles yellow corn meal.

Semolina is also hard to get. People don't know about using it, so no one sells it. KingArthurFlour.com has it as well, and price has gone even higher than the flour ($5.95 two months ago, now **$<u>7.50</u>** for a <u>3</u>-pound bag). Item #3429:

http://www.kingarthurflour.com/shop/detail.jsp?id=3429

You might be able to get semolina at your local supermarket or, more likely, at a specialty store or health-food store.

3. YEAST

This is an item seriously glossed over by chefs and cookbooks. You can spend a fortune on those tiny bags of yeast at the supermarket, or order a one-pound bag of professional yeast on the Internet: **SAF® "RED" INSTANT YEAST.**

They say it's the world's top-selling instant yeast: Another trade secret and *way* cheaper than little packets. It comes vacuum-packed which makes it feel of a solid brick, but as soon as you cut it open, it relaxes and reveals granulated yeast inside.

Of course KingArthurFlour.com has it, so you might as well order all three together. Order three times as much flour as semolina with the one-pound package of yeast:

http://www.kingarthurflour.com/shop/detail.jsp?id=1458

Once you cut open the bag it's unusable, so be sure to get a container *ahead of time* like the one recommended above.

4. OTHER INGREDIENTS

WATER AT 120°

SUGAR

SALT (I USE LOW SODIUM SALT)

<u>REGULAR</u> OLIVE OIL

MOZZARELLA

PROVOLONE (OPTIONAL)

5. MISCELLANEOUS

2-GALLON BAGGIES® PLASTIC BAGS FOR 18" THIN-CRUST PIZZAS (OR 1-GAL FOR SMALLER)

Here
is how to make *real*
professional pizza dough

(not including topings...yet). These recipes were determined after 10 years of testing and experience (and many more years of eating :). **My favorite is the large 18" traditional NYC Italian-style thin-crust pizza.** I'll also give you the recipes for Chicago-style deep-dish pizza as well as several different sizes. All have the same ingredients and proportions, just different multiplication factors. However, I'll not require you do the multiplication on your own; I'll give you the numbers.

Feel free to experiment on your own, and if you think you can improve on these recipes, let me know. But the consensus is that these recipes result in professional pizzas that are beyond delicious.

You probably should measure-out your ingredients while on these pages, because later I'll be referencing the 18 thin-crust pizza only. Use an accurate scale and accurate measuring spoons (level measuring). The little glass bowls are for temporarily holding some ingredients.

1. LARGE (18"), NYC ITALIAN THIN-CRUST

10 oz **HIGH-GLUTEN FLOUR**
(weigh it and throw into the stand mixer bowl)

3.7 oz **SEMOLINA**
(weigh it and throw into the stand mixer bowl)

8.0 oz (by *weight*) **WATER*** at 120°
(keep water running at 120° until ready to weigh)

5 tsp **SUGAR** plus 1¼ tsp **SUGAR** *for the mixer bowl*

[½+⅛] tsp **SALT** plus [½+⅛] tsp **SALT** *for the mixer bowl*

1¼ tsp <u>**REGULAR**</u> **OLIVE OIL**

2 tsp SAF RED **INSTANT YEAST**

*At this time, there is no way to confirm that NYC water makes a difference.

2. MEDIUM (16") THIN-CRUST PIZZA OR 12" DEEP-DISH PIZZA

8 oz HIGH-GLUTEN FLOUR
(weigh it and throw into the stand mixer bowl)

3 oz SEMOLINA
(weigh it and throw into the stand mixer bowl)

6.4 oz (by _weight_) WATER* at 120°
(keep water running at 120° until ready to weigh)

4 tsp SUGAR plus 1 tsp SUGAR *for the mixer bowl*

½ tsp SALT plus ½ tsp SALT *for the mixer bowl*

1 tsp **REGULAR** OLIVE OIL

1½ tsp SAF RED **INSTANT YEAST**

(BE SURE TO USE ONLY VERY FRESH INGREDIENTS.)

*At this time, there is no way to confirm that NYC water makes a difference.

3. LARGE (18") DEEP-DISH PIZZA
(ARE YOU SURE YOU HAVE THE ROOM?)

18 oz HIGH-GLUTEN FLOUR

(weigh it and throw into the stand mixer bowl)

6.8 oz SEMOLINA

(weigh it and throw into the stand mixer bowl)

14.4 oz (by *weight*) WATER* at 120°

(keep water running at 120° until ready to weigh)

9 tsp **SUGAR** plus 2¼ tsp **SUGAR** *for the mixer bowl*

1⅛ tsp **SALT** plus 1⅛ tsp **SALT** *for the mixer bowl*

2¼ tsp **REGULAR** OLIVE OIL

3½ tsp SAF RED **INSTANT YEAST**

(BE SURE TO USE ONLY VERY FRESH INGREDIENTS.)

*At this time, there is no way to confirm that NYC water makes a difference.

Pizza is made in two main steps: First you **make the dough** 4.5–10.5–26.5 hours in advance, then you **make the pizza**. So you must do a little advance planning. Basically, if you're going to serve pizza for dinner tomorrow night, make the dough the night before...but plan for a _**half-hour**_ of dough prep followed by _**2 hours**_ rising on the counter. After that, you will put it in the refrigerator and walk away for up to 24 hours before making the pizza (_**another 30-60 minutes**_). Alternatively, you can make the dough early in the morning and put it into the refrigerator and walk away for up to 8 hours. (If you need pizza much sooner, you can get away with 2 hours in the refrigerator but it will be less excellent in the end. Some say you can make the dough and freeze it after the first 2-24 hours in the refrigerator, but I wouldn't.) For the purpose of simplicity, I'm going to refer to the 18" thin-crust pizza from here on. At the end, I'll discuss the deep-dish pizza.

1. RUN WATER AT 120° INTO ANY CUP

Other recipes will tell you this is too hot and will kill the yeast. It won't because by the time you use it, it will cool down to the proper temperature (110°-115°).

2. MEASURE SALTS, SUGARS, & YEAST

Using your measuring spoons and 5 small ingredient bowls, **dole out:**
- 5 tsp sugar,
- ½+⅛ tsp salt
- 2 tsp Inst. Yeast
- 1¼ tsp sugar
- another ½+⅛ tsp salt

3. HEAT THE MIXER BOWL

Run some 120° water in the mixer bowl to heat it and then **dry** with a paper towel.

4. WEIGH* FLOUR AND SEMOLINA

Place 3-cup container on the scale. Use scooper to **scoop out** 10 oz flour and 3.7 oz semolina. **Weigh** _separately_ & **dump** into mixer bowl.

5. DUMP THESE 2 DRY INGREDIENTS INTO THE MIXER BOWL

6. WHISK THE DRY INGREDIENTS IN THE MIXER BOWL

Then **place on stand, attach** dough hook, **raise bowl** to full height, set mixer to **speed 2.**

7. WEIGH* THE WATER

Place 1-cup measuring cup on the scale, reset to 0, and **pour** 120° water into the cup until the scale reads 8 oz. It's the only way to get the **exact** amount of water.

8. DISSOLVE YEAST, SUGAR, SALT, AND OIL

Remove measuring cup from the scale. Into the measuring cup with 8 oz water **dump** your premeasured
- 5 tsp SUGAR
- ½+⅛ tsp SALT
- 1¼ tsp *regular olive oil*

Start stirring this mixture (with the 1 tsp measuring spoon) and then **dump** in the premeasured
- 2 tsp Inst. Yeast

Stir for **one minute**, until all the yeast is dissolved. (Use back of spoon to squish lumps against side of cup.)

9. DUMP THE WATER MIXTURE INTO THE MIXER BOWL WITH DRY INGREDIENTS ON SPEED 2

MIX on speed 2 for **one minute**. Dough will form and pull away from the sides of the bowl.

*WHEN WEIGHING WITH A RECEPTACLE, BE SURE TO ZERO OUT THE SCALE ("TARE" FUNCTION) AFTER PLACING THE MEASURING RECEPTACLE ON THE SCALE. THIS ALLOWS YOU TO WEIGH ONLY THE CONTENTS OF THE RECEPTACLE.

10. KNEAD THE DOUGH: SET MIXER TO SPEED 1 FOR 20 MINUTES

Place the 1-cup container under the mixer bowl and drop the bowl halfway down so the bowl sits on the container. This prevents the dough from riding around on the hook without being kneaded and why you need a bowl-lift mixer. If you have a tilt-head mixer you can't do this, so you'll have to check the dough every couple of minutes. If it's going for a ride you'll have to stop the mixer and pull the dough off the hook (maybe not if you have the newer spiral dough hook, see page 14). (Even using my halfway-down method, some dough might sneak up the hook.) (BTW...The KitchenAid manual gives entirely different directions; forget about it.)

At the end of the cycle the dough will be *slightly* sticky and should leave a little residue on your hands.

KEEP AN EYE ON THE KNEADING

11. IN THE MEANTIME (WHILE THE DOUGH IS KNEADING), YOU SHOULD DO **3** THINGS: A. PREPARE FOR RISING THE DOUGH; B. SHRED THE MOZZARELLA (AND OPTIONAL PROVOLONE); C. MAKE THE SAUCE (ANY TIME, BUT COOL IT OFF) (RECIPE P. 31)

A. Prepare a 2-gallon plastic bag (1-gallon for smaller pizzas) for the rising of the dough: Spoon two heaping teaspoons of high-gluten flour into the bag and **shake** thoroughly to coat the bag lightly. Then **shake out the excess** back into the flour container.
B. Shred 12 oz cheese (8–12 oz mozzarella + **0**-4 oz provolone...or more) in the food processor with grater attachment or use a heavy-duty cheese grater. (Using mozzarella alone is creamier; adding provolone makes it a little chewier. I prefer mozzarella alone, so I do half the pizza that way. For an 18" pizza, 12 oz total cheese is medium.)

12. REMOVE BOWL

After 20 minutes, **stop** the mixer (*very important* :), lift the bowl, **remove** the 1-cup container under the bowl, then **drop** the bowl. **Detach** the dough hook with the dough, **drop** into the mixer bowl, **remove** bowl with hook+dough.

13. REMOVE DOUGH / FORM A BALL

Hold the dough in both hands, thumbs in the middle and towards you. **Spread** the top surface of the dough apart with your thumbs and palms to the left and right while the rest of your fingers underneath **push** the dough into itself and **seal** the bottom. Do this 3 or 4 times, turning 'round and 'round, forming a **nice, tight ball**.

14. PLACE THE DOUGH IN THE PLASTIC BAG · · · · ·

On your kitchen counter, in a warm place, place the dough ball in the plastic bag toward the back, leaving plenty of room for expansion. (It will **way more than double**.) And then fold the open end of the bag under the edge of the dough, somewhat "sealing" the bag closed and centering the dough.

FOR 2 HOURS

15. LAY A KITCHEN TOWEL OVER THE DOUGH TO KEEP IT WARM FOR 2 HOURS

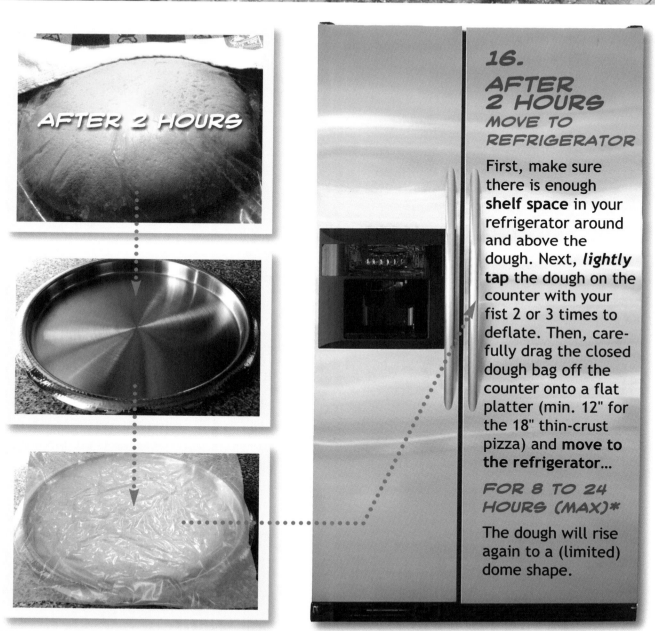

AFTER 2 HOURS

16.
AFTER 2 HOURS
MOVE TO REFRIGERATOR

First, make sure there is enough **shelf space** in your refrigerator around and above the dough. Next, *lightly tap* the dough on the counter with your fist 2 or 3 times to deflate. Then, carefully drag the closed dough bag off the counter onto a flat platter (min. 12" for the 18" thin-crust pizza) and **move to the refrigerator...**

FOR 8 TO 24 HOURS (MAX)*

The dough will rise again to a (limited) dome shape.

*AGAIN, YOU CAN GET AWAY WITH A MINIMUM OF 2 HOURS IN THE REFRIGERATOR, BUT THE DOUGH WON'T BAKE OR TASTE AS GOOD AND CONSISTENT.

HERE IS MY ULTIMATE PIZZA AND PASTA SAUCE. IT'S AVAILABLE IN SEVERAL VARIATIONS, BUT HERE I'M GIVING YOU JUST THE ONE BEST FOR PIZZA. IT CAN ALSO BE USED AS A GREAT MARINARA SAUCE FOR PASTA. RICHER SAUCE VARIATIONS WILL BE IN A FUTURE MANUAL. ALL ARE CHEAPER, EASIER, AND BETTER THAN ANY READY-MADE BOTTLED SAUCE FOR PASTA OR PIZZA! (BE SURE TO USE ONLY VERY FRESH INGREDIENTS.)

29 oz can **RED PACK® PUREE**
(You can use any puree but flavor __will__ be different.)

1¾ cups **WATER*** *(or half of the puree can)*

3 TBS **SUGAR**
*(Adjust this ↕ if you are **not** using Red Pack Puree.)*

1 tsp **SALT**

1 heaping tsp **CRUSHED DRIED SWEET BASIL**

½ heaping tsp **CRUSHED DRIED OREGANO**

¼ tsp black **PEPPER**

3 cubes **CHICKEN-FLAVOR BOUILLON**
(Wyler's® brand recommended / OPTIONAL)

⅛ cup **KETCHUP**
(Heinz® brand recommended / OPTIONAL)

½ tsp **ASIAN CHILE PASTE**
(Caution: VERY HOT!...add more or less __or none__)

PROCEDURE: __THROW EVERYTHING__ INTO A 4-QUART POT, BRING TO A __BOIL__, THEN __SIMMER__ FOR 10-15 MINUTES, __STIRRING__ EVERY FOUR MINUTES.

THE ULTIMATE PIZZA / PASTA SAUCE

At this time, there is no way to confirm that the kind of water makes a difference.

FIFTH: PREP THE OVEN

AFTER 8-24 HOURS...

SCREEN IS ALLOWED TO TOUCH
BACK OF THE OVEN AND TO HANG
OVER THE FRONT OF THE RACK
TO TOUCH THE FRONT DOOR

OVEN RACK IS UPSIDE-DOWN AND
BACKWARDS TO PERMIT MAXIMUM
TOP SURFACE FOR SCREEN

THIS OVEN IS 19" FROM DOOR TO BACK, PERFECT
FOR A 19" SCREEN. TO MEASURE YOURS, PULL THE RACK
OUT AND CLOSE THE DOOR ON IT. THEN MEASURE FROM
CENTER BACK OF OVEN TO FRONT OF RACK

PREHEAT OVEN TO 475°

REMOVE ALL OTHER RACKS

DO NOT PLACE THE SCREEN IN THE OVEN FOR PREHEATING.

IT IS SHOWN HERE ONLY TO DEMONSTRATE POSITIONING

TOP OF RACK IS ABOUT 4" FROM THE BOTTOM OF THE OVEN

*** REMOVE OVEN LINER ***

(YOUR OVEN MIGHT DIFFER.)

SIXTH: TIME TO MAKE THE PIZZA

WHILE OVEN PREHEATS...

17. PREPARE FOR FORMING THE CRUST

Place a 12" strip of a non-skid mat on the counter under your pizza peel;

Add 2 TBS of **semolina** to the peel and spread around the entire peel (no, not the handle);

Remove the platter with the dough from the refrigerator;

Open the plastic dough bag and cut the top open from the open side to closed side and then from left to right across the closed side;

Wrap the bag flaps around the bottom of the platter and **flip the platter over** to dump the dough onto center of the semolina on the peel.

NOTES: 1) IT'S EVEN BETTER TO PLACE THE DOUGH RIGHT-SIDE UP ON THE PEEL, SO TRY FIRST FLIPPING IT GENTLY ONTO ANOTHER PLATE AND CUT THE BAG ON THE BOTTOM.
2) AFTER PLACING THE DOUGH ON THE PEEL YOU SHOULD NEVER HAVE A PROBLEM WITH THE DOUGH STICKING TO THE PEEL BECAUSE OF THE SEMOLINA. DON'T ADD FLOUR TO THE PEEL.

NON-SKID MAT (ONLY NEEDS TO BE A 12" STRIP)

18. START SHAPING THE CRUST

Pressing with the tips of your fingers, **spread** the dough outward and to the left and right, while **turning** the dough for about a minute, until it is about 14" in diameter. **Maintain** a nice, even circle. The dough will be fairly elastic and might spring back. Let it **rest** and try again. Occasionally **lift** around the edges and **sweep semolina** back under the dough.

Expand from **12"** to **14"**

AVOID PRESSING THE OUTER 1" EDGE TO KEEP IT THICKER.

19. LIFT AND STRETCH

While I'm not going to suggest that you spend the next 30 minutes abusing the dough by spreading it out to 18" with your finger tips (please don't use a rolling pin either), I'm also not going to recommend that you start spinning the dough in the air like a professional pizza-maker to save time. (It's **very** difficult even if you do have the physical space to do it.) But if you do the following, you might graduate towards that...

Keeping your pizza serving tray nearby, lift the dough and carry it over the knuckles of both hands over to the pizza tray. Hovering **_over_** the tray (in case you drop the dough and _you will_ drop semolina), just let the dough hang from your knuckles and spread itself using gravity. (Stay away from the center of the dough and don't let the dough touch the tray.) _AND,_ **hopping** up and down **_gently_**, **ROTATE the dough** so it spreads evenly. You're only going to be able to do this for maybe 10 seconds but it helps a lot. Then carefully **lay it back down on the _peel_**. Try not to get semolina on the top of the dough and **DO NOT** let the top of the dough stick to itself.

20. KEEP STRETCHING

Still more to go: On the peel, with palms up, use your fingers to go **around and around UNDER** the dough, **lifting and stretching,** _avoiding the thinner center and thicker 1" edge_, until the dough almost hangs over the edge of the peel (not shown). Occasionally **sweep semolina back under** the dough.

21. DOCK AND PINCH

Slowly **dock** the dough (straight across in rows is fine). This helps the dough bake through and through. Then **go around** the outer edge **pinching** about ½" of the dough to make a ridge. Go around a couple of times to make sure it's not "pinchy-looking." This will help give a nicely formed, professional, soft, and chewy edge to the finished pizza.

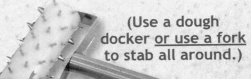

(Use a dough docker <u>or use a fork</u> to stab all around.)

22. POSITION EXPANDABLE SINK STRAINER OVER THE SINK, AND...

(IF YOU'RE REALLY PRE-PARED, YOU'LL HAVE THE STRAINER & SCREEN OVER THE SINK BEFORE FORMING THE DOUGH ON THE PEEL. AND PLEASE...TURN OFF THE WATER ;-)

...PLACE 19" SCREEN OVER EXPANDABLE SINK STRAINER

(THE SINK STRAINER LETS EXCESS SEMOLINA FALL INTO THE SINK, BUT IF YOU CAN'T DO THIS, PUT THE SCREEN FLAT ON YOUR COUNTERTOP.)

USE SHORT JABS TO SLIDE THE DOUGH OFF THE PEEL ONTO THE SCREEN. WHEN THE PEEL IS ABOUT 1/3 TO 1/2 OUT, PULL OUT QUICKLY ALL THE WAY. MIGHT TAKE PRACTICE.

YOUR PIZZA DOUGH IS NOT GOING TO LAND PERFECTLY ROUND (IT WASN'T TO BEGIN WITH) AND WILL SHRINK FROM SHAKING THE PEEL. YOU NEED TO FIX IT (NEXT PAGE).

22. SLIDE DOUGH ONTO THE SCREEN

23. WITH PALMS UP, USE YOUR FINGERS AGAIN TO STRETCH UNDERNEATH THE OUTER 2-4" OF DOUGH TO MEET THE EDGES OF THE PIZZA SCREEN.

VOILA! YOUR PIZZA WILL BE

PERFECTLY ROUND!

AND A FULL 19"!

(ALTHOUGH IT WILL SHRINK A LITTLE IN THE OVEN.)

24. "DRESS" THE PIZZA DOUGH

Put 2 TBS of REGULAR OLIVE OIL + ½ tsp SALT to a small ingredient bowl. Stir well. ◄•••►

Using the tips of your fingers of one hand to pick up oil+salt, **gently wipe the oil+salt** all over the pizza dough to about 1" from the outer edge, which will have no oil and no sauce.

This will add flavor and texture, but *more importantly, it will prevent the sauce from soaking into the dough and enable the dough to bake through.*

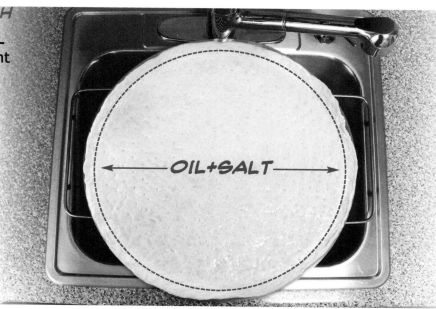

—OIL+SALT—

25. APPLY COOLED SAUCE

Use the ladle (or a large serving spoon) to **apply about 1¼ cup of SAUCE** up to 1" from the outer edge, which will have no sauce.

Spread out in circular motion with the back of the ladle or spoon.

You're almost ready to bake!

26. ADD THE CHEESE(S)

Sprinkle evenly the cheese(s)—mozzarella and the optional provolone—which you previously shredded. Again, avoid the outer 1" margin of the dough. (Extra cheese pictured.)

Season with some salt and fresh pepper and possibly crushed, dried oregano.

You're ready to bake!

YOU CAN ADD OTHER TOPPINGS, LIKE PEPPERONI OR <u>COOKED CHOPPED MEAT OR SAUSAGE (FAT DRAINED AND COOLED)</u>, BUT USE LOW-MOISTURE ITEMS AND KEEP IT LIGHT— IT WON'T COOK PROPERLY.

27. PLACE SCREEN WITH PREPPED PIZZA IN 475° OVEN

Here's the easy part. Rather than trying to slide the pizza from a peel onto a hot stone or screen in the oven at ankle height, just **pick up the screen** with the pizza **and place** centered on the oven rack. **Close** the door quickly.

Bake for 7 to 8+ minutes according to taste. (Check after 7 minutes.)

SCREEN GOES OVER RAISED CROSSBARS ON RACK

PREP OVEN AS SHOWN ON PAGES 32-33 & BE SURE TO REMOVE OVEN LINER!

7$\frac{1}{2}$-8 MINUTES
AT 475°

28. CRISPING AND COOLING

Unless you choose to over bake the pizza, merely baking the pizza in a gas oven for 7½ to 8 minutes (or longer, if you like) is usually not enough to make the bottom crackingly crispy (unless you have an electric convection oven with exposed element on the bottom). (The semolina on the crust will make it seem pleasantly crunchy, either way.)

If you *do* want the bottom crispier after removal from the oven, **put the pizza+ screen on a large electric grill for 1-2 minutes**. Move around if it doesn't fit.

If not, skip it and go directly to **cooling:** With the sink strainer on the counter, put the pizza+screen on top for about 30 seconds, until the cheese stops bubbling.

In the meantime, very low heat the pizza serving tray over two stovetop burners for 30 seconds.

29. CUTTING

Lift the HOT pizza+screen and slide the pizza off onto the HOT 19" pizza serving tray. The tray will be bigger than the pizza, making it easy to cut from edge to edge.

Cut across the center with the pizza wheel. Rotate 90° and cut across the center again. Do two more cuts across in-between the other two cuts. (See page 8.) Do this quickly as the longer the pizza stays on the tray, the soggier it gets.

This is why you want to want to quickly **slide the cut slices right back onto the screen** for serving.

Carry the screen on the sink strainer to the table. Keeping it on the strainer will maintain air flow and a better, non-soggy crust.

Refrigerate leftovers for up to one week. You can also freeze leftovers much longer—*IF* you can resist.

30. REHEATING FOR MAXIMUM GOODNESS

You can use one of two methods for reheating: a) you can use the **toaster oven** set to "high toast" (top and bottom heating) and optionally hit it for a **second time on low**. Or, b) for crispier pizza, place the cold slice(s) *upside-down* on a broiler tray in the oven on a rack about **5" from the top broiler element** on high for 5 minutes. **Then flip it over** for another minute on low. (**If** the oven or toaster oven is **already hot** reduce the times and monitor.) (Use the microwave *only* for [minimal] defrosting; pizza will get rubbery if you use it for heating.)

THICKER, FLUFFIER THIN-CRUST PIZZA

After forming the dough on the pizza screen (before adding the oil+salt), **let the dough rise on the screen** for 20-25 minutes, untouched. You want the dough to puff up, so **be gentle** when adding the oil+salt, sauce, and cheese.

THINNER THIN-CRUST PIZZA

Let the dough rise on the counter for **3¼ hours** instead of 2 hours. The dough will pretty much exhaust its rising to ensure a flatter, extra-thin crust. Gently tap down and refrigerate as before.

12" THIN-CRUST PIZZAS

Divide the dough in two for a 16" pizza (thinner) or for an 18" pizza (thicker) **by weight** (or by eye) before refrigerating.

12" DEEP-DISH PAN PIZZA

12" pan pizza is *much easier*, if you prefer, and able to take on more toppings. After refrigeration, put the dough into a slightly oiled 12" deep-dish pizza pan. With your fingers spread out to fill the pan and form a ½"-high "wall" of dough around the wall of the pan. **Poke holes** with a fork. Coat the dough with the oil+salt and top with [less] sauce and cheese, leaving a ½" gap from the wall.) **Bake at 475° for 7 to 8 minutes** or more, **judging by the darkness** of the crust. Use a **spatula to remove** the finished pizza from the pan and **place** on a pizza screen.

EXTRA SPECIAL TOPPINGS

Experiment! Top with pepperoni, cooked sausage, cooked beef, peppers, olives, onions, mushrooms, anchovies, and even ham and pineapple before baking. But there is one topping that I don't think anyone has ever discovered, and in my opinion it's truly "to-die-for:" *GUACAMOLE.* Spread cool guacamole on a hot slice before enjoying. Its ingredients complement pizza *wonderfully!* (Important note: My next cookbook has the ultimate guacamole recipe!)

EVERYONE LOVES PIZZA!
HERE IS YOUR CHANCE TO MAKE
THE ULTIMATE THIN-CRUST PIZZA
RIGHT IN YOUR OWN HOME...AS
REWARDING AS IT IS DELICIOUS!

MANGIA!

Francesco Brunaldo

Printed in the United States
154705LV00002B